A Living God

Roshan B. Karki

ISBN: 9798836150464

DEDICATION

To my wife Roshina.

CONTENTS

Acknowledgments   i

1   Poems about Mythical Subjects   3

2   Poems about life and other subjects   Pg 8

3   Poems about my wife Roshina   Pg 20

4   Poems about Love   Pg 30

5   Poems about me   Pg 35

6   Poems about writings   Pg 45

ACKNOWLEDGMENTS

POEMS ABOUT MYTHICAL SUBJECTS

An Angel

White feathers
Made of velvet
White in colors
Eyelashes black
With black eye linings
As if it is made in heaven

Heart soft
Flying in the skies
Visible to few eyes
I am one of them.
I am an angel

My Guitar

I have not touched my guitars for years.
There is no doubt why it is in tears.
Cause few years we were peers.
I used to keep my guitar near me before sleeping.

My guitar had a secret chord
and I used to play it to Gods
living in seven layers of heaven.
But the Gods envied me and my guitar
as I played it more beautifully then anything on the
earth.

So they cursed my guitar.
The stings came out and it went old.
I play it no more.
It's lying in the corner
where it is sleeping and weeping.

Roaming with Ghost riders

I saw a herd of ghost riders
as the moon was passing by.
It was burning with fire and fumes.
The night was about to cry.

The villages and people were deep in sleep.
the leader came to me and said,
"We work for justice. We work for Lord.
Here is my herd,"

He offered me a ride.
The horses were burning.
I looked at village from way up
the village looked as if it is frosted.

Before the night vanished
smoke rose to heaven
And before it was dawn
the ghost riders vanished.

I am still waiting for the Ghost riders to pass by
but they might be inside seven layers of heaven.

Second layer of Heaven

An angle guided to me second layer of heaven.
There were temples, churches and mosques.
There were kind people with warm hearts.
There are butterflies and peaceful birds.

Soon we came to a place where Buddha was
meditating.
Allah was chanting syllables.
Jesus was playing harp.
Krishna was flying kites.

And we reached a laboratory
where dreams were made.
It was a factory where
Couples were designed.

A signboard said, "The goal of life
is to reach heaven.
The no layers of heaven are seven.
So don't be stubborn and
head to the layers of heaven."

Sound of the Sea

Its midnight
yet the waves are dancing.
There is a different world on the beach.
Listen to the sound of the sea.

May be the waves do not feel tired.
The ship is on the horizon.
The freedom bells are ringing.
Listen to the sound of the sea.

The lovers quiet and thirsty
are on the beach.
They must feel romantic
listening to the sound of the sea.

The lighthouse is all lit up.
Hear the heartbeat of the sea.
The nymphs may be dancing
listening to the sound of the sea.

POEMS ABOUT LIFE AND OTHER SUBJECTS

A Fiction

What's life?
A fiction
I do not know
what's coming.

What's life?
A story
I write everyday
each day is a metaphor.

What's life?
A poetry
I can feel
when you are by my side.

A Fiction

What's life?
A fiction
I do not know
what's coming.

What's life?
A story
I write everyday
each day is a metaphor.

What's life?
A poetry
I can feel
when you are by my side.

Abraham Lincoln

Failures, failures, failures
I have never seen what success is like.
Chop trees on twilight.
Practice law for the poor.
My Abraham Lincoln! My hero!
You saved the world from cruelty and pain.
History will remember you and your presidency
even in the millenniums to come.

Bars

Your charm burns beautifully
as if you are a star
flying across distant constellations
as we grab a drink in a bar.

The bar is always crowded
even in the week days.
Because when we grab a drink
you glitter like stars.

The talk fills the room
and it will be morning soon.
Let the night remember us
as we hit the crowded bars.

Hollywood Hill

There are lots of hills
that should be conquered
and Hollywood hill is one of them.
The pride of western culture
lies tall, green and erect.

It represents U.S Royalties
who work hard for
themselves and the people.
The passion is burning like fire.

Each creative person should
see holly wood hill
and mark footprints on it.

In Every Sunsets

I will walk to top of hill
and climb the tree
where we used to meet
to see every sunsets.

Where is the sun?
And where have you gone?
You have passed away like
Rain on the mountains
Like glaciers in the sea
Like thunder in the sky

But the moon
Pale and yellow
Gives me hope

Where is the sun?
And where have you gone?
You have passed away like
rain on the mountains.

Map of the World

I see a beggar
with wrinkles
and untold stories.
I wonder how has he
ended up here
relying on the pity of the world.
He keeps an account of
how many people passed by
and how many of them were generous .
His face has map of the world.

On the Way the Bird Flew

On the way the bird flew
I looked at it as far as my sight could.
Probably it was aiming for heaven or the moon.
It was about to get dark soon.

I wanted to fly like the bird
but I have no wings to do so.
So I looked at the bird
until it disappeared in the twilight.

But it cannot talk like me.
It cannot cook for me.
We have something special about us.
But I could not stop looking at the bird that flew.

The Destiny is calling

Did you hear the bell chime my friends?
It's ringing from heaven to down below.
Some of us will be doctors.
Some of us will be lawyers.
Cause the destiny is calling.

Make no mistake and go forth.
Hear the ring of bells. Hear the Lord's words.
We will bring happiness in the world.
Cause the bell is ringing.

The destiny is calling.

The Horizon

The moon is in the horizon
but the horizon is in tears
I wonder why it is crying.

May be its crying cause
People who aim at horizon are few
You need a strong boat to reach horizon.
The horizon is all black and blue.

Someday I will reach their
breaking the entire barrier.
And I will ask both the horizon and the moon
"Why was it crying? "

The Search

I have been searching
like you have been.
We have been searching
in vacant streets and crowded bars.

When will we find it?
We should. We must
at any cost.
We should keep up the search.

There are gold mines
and beautiful statues on earth.
Someday we will find it.
We should keep up the search.

Wall of my Heart

Meaningless roads lead me there.
Day by day the road is getting stranger.
It leads to a church where you can pray.
Faith is a strong thing some people say.

Jesus must be watching from heaven.
The church is a home to me now.
The road of faith is covered with thorns.
The walls of the church are paved with stones.

\------------------

********************* _________________________________

  ****
__

Drink some wine for it's my tear now.
I have been praying since you are gone.
The bread is my food now
and faith is my job.

Will Jesus from heaven make you come back?
I doubt it but I can't stop praying him.
People say he can create miracles.
I wish he has seen me in tears.

For the road is covered with thorns.
The wall of my heart is paved with stones.

POEMS ABOUT MY WIFE ROSHINA

All we need for Now

The river has beauty
while we row down it together.
The oars are our hands
as we paddle down on boat.

Each sunrise and sunsets are proofs
we have rowed down the boat.
The waves are higher powers or Gods
that will be in our life.

We will feed on fresh fishes.
We will be together
until the sea and boat will be there.
We will pray sea god.

This is all we need for now.

As we hit the Club

The moon will be hiding
and discotheque lights will be on sight.
Let us pass this night
with dance and wine.
It will be wonderful tonight.
We will hit the club tonight.

Let the DJ bring out his best work.
You put your hands on mine
and we will go gentle tonight.
We will go forth with wine and shots.
We will hit the club tonight.

Tonight is the proof we are young.
We are thirsty for love this night.
Let there be joy and beats
as we hit he club tonight.

Beautiful Nights

The moon is in the sky
and you are by my side.
The night has beauty in it.
It's a beautiful night.

The moon is asleep.
The forests are dark and deep.
Let the trees whisper to each other.
It's a beautiful night.

The process starts with a kiss.
Soon the bliss of love will be in the room
as we lay in bedroom
looking at the moon on horizon.

Let's not waste a single second.
It's a beautiful night.

Cast Spell Once Again

Daylights are suitable to make love
as I will see you more clearly.
Your beauty is like nothing on earth.
Let me kiss you and start the magic.

No magicians can create magic like I do.
I will cast a spell on you.
I will examine you like a doctor.
Let there be love. Let there be laughter.

No magicians can create magic like I do.
Let me cast a spell on you.

Everyday are fairytales

I believe in God.
I believe in ferries.
You and I are creating
wonderful stories.
The sun and the moon
roam on the skies
on our commands.
The lord from the heaven
will fulfill our vows.
When we are together
the breeze flows swiftly.
The rain falls on the seas.
I am grateful to gods.
Cause everyday is a fairytale.

My Sweet Lady

My sweet lady
what makes you so sweet?
Is it a bar of chocolate
or is it my kiss?
Is it a cocktail drink
or is it some spiritual bliss?
My sweet lady
what makes you so sweet?

My sweet lady
what makes you so sweet?
Is it a star in a distance?
Or is it the moon?
Because your sweetness is
a beautiful trance I can listen to everyday.
I wonder what makes you so sweet.

My Wish for you

My love may you grow
tender with years
May your beauty
grow like flowers

May you love me
and be loved by me
We are paddling a boat
in a distant sea

May rain drop on your face
and kiss the sea.
May life be a flower
and you are a bee.

May you never feel lonely
and light my life daily
My wishes for you are like purest diamonds.
May you shine like it

Show me what Love is

You have shown what love is
when I was left ignored.
I was weeping in a corner.
You held me hand and healed it like god.

I am in a way to win the world.
You are my Josephine and I am Napoleon Bonaparte.
The nymphs will sing and kids will make stories
because you have shown me what love is.

 And we will be together for hundreds of years.
You are my queen and our children will be heirs.
We will pass every difficulty whatever it is
because you have shown what love is.

Valentine's Day

Each Valentine
I will buy you a present
so we can get warm
in cold winter days.

What is a rose?
A frosted plant
in the garden with snow
The Valentine day must be
there so can get better use of it.

Waste no time
Gift your valentine
Life never comes back
but winter does.

Wherever you go

(Inspired by Nepali song" Jaha Jaha janchau timi" by Aruna Lama)

Wherever you go
I will follow you
through dusk or dawn.
Through the sun or the bleeding moon
Through happiness and sorrow
I will follow your footsteps
Through lakes or the swamps
Through youth or old age
Even I have to become a sage
Our life will be a fairytale
I feel so fortunate
As we walk the path of life
Through rusts and gold mine
I will follow you wherever you go
I will be your footsteps
Let me be your footsteps

POEMS ABOUT LOVE

An Oath

Living is an oath.
Each day I fulfill
my promises
and fulfilling oaths is easy
when you are by my side
and it's worth it.

The butterfly
fulfills the oath of a cocoon.
A soldier
fulfills the oath of his lover.

And my oath is to
grow old with you
sharing happiness and sorrow
and be always by your side.

Bless us with Abundance

My Lord! Bless us with abundance.
Let lepers heal and life be
beautiful trance everyone can listen to.
Lord! Bless us with love and gratitude.
Let humanity go to higher altitude.

Let us hug each others with feelings of brotherhood.
Let there be trees and breeze.
Let the flowers blossom with their colors.
Cause you are everything.
Bless us with abundance.

How much the Heart Weights

My lovers please tell me
how much my heart weights?
A pound or less than that
You should know it
You have been in and out of there.
You have seen my love
and when you are not there
you have seen my tears.
It's all yours now my love.
Tell me how much my heart weights.

Island and the Sea

There's an island
not habited
lying alone and crying alone
and a sea surrounds it.

Beautiful roses grow
on the island.
The water from the sea
nurtures it.

Unknown creatures
lay on the beach of the island
and make love.
The sea knows it.

But the unknown creatures
do not know what rose is.
But the island and the sea are friends and
they will cherish the roses
crying alone and lying alone
by the sea.

Last night before War

Tomorrow, before you wake up
I will get dressed and head to war.
But I will not let you know that
so kiss me till be lungs are full.
Feel every inch of me.

But I will leave a note for you
so that you can dwell in memories.
Someday I will come back for you.
The horse is ready
so is the saddle.

It might be few months or year
before I will come back.
We will make more love after that.

It's our last night before war.

POEMS ABOUT ME

A Living God

My friend let me tell you
I feel I am a living God.
I have done miracles
and my third eye sees divine colors.

I see exact colors.
Behind the heads of Hindu Gods.
I am supernatural
I fight war for the good.

You may not believe me
I have my psychedelic states
which turned me into a living God.
I see angels in sky.
I see 11:11 every time I look at the watch.

Why don't you call me for interviews?
Why do not my books sell?
Because I am special
I am a living god.
I will make a better world.

Commanding U.S Troops

The angels give me vision
and I go deep in thoughts.
To come with perfect strategy,
for living I command U.S Troops.

Does my lover know it?
I doubt. And even in sleep
I command U.S troops.
It's work of heaven.

Let my lover know it
I can't explain how
She will feel proud
Knowing I command U.S troops

I am with U.S and its people
until the end of life.
I will command U.S troops.

Inside my Mind

I have dwelled inside my mind
to seek solution and to seek answers.
There are angels and beautiful things
that belong to humanity and heaven.

There is garden and house in my mind.
The garden is full of roses.
You and I stay in the house
making love every day.

And we will walk inside my mind
looking at terracotta's, and pyramids.
There are lakes and parks.
There is a temple and statue.

Did I say it right?
"There is a heaven in my mind."

Man of my Words

I have always been leading.
I lead the world for living.
I fight against evil. I make world better.
You can trust me. I am a man of my words

I have made thousand promises.
I have fulfilled them all.
Leading is my job.
And I am man of my words.

With every letters, with every word
I make world better.
I fulfill my words. I fulfill my vows.
Because I am man of my words

My Special Force

My special force represents the US.
We are on to hundreds.
Honor the charge we make
for Christ's sake, we will
win the war making no mistakes.
The heaven is taking our tests.

God of death will ride with us
using tools of mass destruction.
At any cost we will win the war.
My special force, follow my words
I will command the war riding a fine war horse.
We are ready to ride any time
at sunrise, sunsets or day breaks.

The enemies will be pushed through
jaws of death.
Hear my words and make no mistakes.
The God of death is with us.
We will win all the wars
until I ride
with my special force
fighting against evil foe.

My Youth

My youth passed like a shooting star.
Did I take pleasure of it?
A little! But there was much pain
as there was difficulty finding a way.

My youths passed like rain on the mountains.
The load was heavy
while I was climbing the mountains.
There was no other way then keep walking

And I have reached somewhere.
It's not the place where my acquaintances wanted me
to be.
But I have reached some place I felt like
the load feels lighter now.

The House on the Hill

There is a house on the hill.
You can rest if you are passing by.
You can find shelter and water.
But you need to bring your own food.
It's yours as well please don t feel shy.

Long ago the house belonged to me.
But I left the house in search for destiny.
I have found my destiny
and I am happy to leave the house to passersby.

I felt I have done something better
with my house and with my life.
The house is standing on the hill.
You can find a shelter if you are passing by.

The Night spoke to me

The night spoke to me
in a calm voice
as a summer breeze
when I lie in balcony working.

The town is sleeping
and it was midnight.
I was still working
in a damp kerosene lamp.

The night said, "My child!
You know the night
and its fruit.
You will be remembered someday."

Bhagavad Gita says,
"Work hard but expect nothing.
Be with then night
and work hard on your crafts."

And I hope it's right
to work in night
under the damp kerosene light.
I want to be remembered someday.
I know the night.

The Woods are my Friends

The woods are my friends
while I am walking alone.
They speak to me in soft breeze.
But do they know my name?

The forest is dense and there is fog.
I want to keep walking and never stop.
The woods speak to me secretly.
They are laden with love. They are laden with
serenity.

May be the leaves quenches their thirst.
Here is beauty and here is trust.
Cause the woods are my friends now
while I am walking along with woods alone

What's living?

I wonder what's living.
Living lies is a bottle for a drunkard.
Living lies in oath to lovers.
Living lies in purity for Buddha's followers.
Living lies in seas, the sun and the moon.
Living lies in walk for toddlers.

And I must be living
in my own world, in my own account.
I write poems. I am a politician.
But I have a little different path then you have taken.

But I too am living
and I feel in a better way.

POEMS ABOUT WRITINGS

A Holiday to write poems

Give me some wine
A fine notebook
A pen, some ink
A place to stand
Some tobacco
Good memories
Your presence
Some shadow
Some warmth
A leisure day
Send me on a holiday
to write poems
and it will be
best holiday ever.

A Vacation

Let me take you to vacation
away from this world to distant constellation.
We will enter wormholes and enter heaven.
We will live up to hundred and eleven.
We will meet gods and know the secrets
the world has seldom seen.
Let us see nymphs and drink with angels.
We will meet fairy creatures and live with them.
We will sing and dance with mermaids.
We will see multidimensional skyscrapers and plane.
Tonight in your dreams let me take you to a vacation.

Ask me what Poetry is

Ask me what poetry is;
It's asking a shadow to dance.
It's auras of the moon.
It's warmth of sun in noon.
It's kiss of lovers.
It's the walk of toddlers.
It's lamentation of a wife
of dead soldiers in her tomb.
It's glitter of dews on sun rays.
I am a poet.
You can ask me what poetry is.

Pen and Ink

The words
floating like clouds
Ink is the river
And pen is sloughing
In white fields
to get fruits
The words are floating
Like feathers

Writing a Book

First comes the title
then comes the content
then comes the cover
then comes the dedication.

Your skin wrinkles.
And it takes few months
and when you complete it,
publish it and read it
you feel it's worth it

ABOUT THE AUTHOR

Roshan B. Karki (Roshan Bikram Kark) is a poet, writer, musician and entrepreneur. He was born in Charikot, Dolkha. He has attended Loras College, USA as a honors student to pursue undergraduate in Creative writing. " A Living God" is sixteenth book by the author. It consists of poems about real life spiritual experiences, love experiences. These poems will entertain you like nothing else.